D0873873

OTHER BOOKS BY MURIEL RUKEYSER

Theory of Flight
U.S. 1
A Turning Wind
Wake Island
Willard Gibbs
Beast in View
The Green Wave
Orpheus
The Life of Poetry
Elegies
Selected Poems
One Life
Body of Waking
Waterlily Fire
The Orgy

TRANSLATIONS

Selected Poems of Octavio Paz
Sun Stone (by Octavio Paz)
Selected Poems of Gunnar Ekelöf (with Leif Sjöberg)

CHILDREN'S BOOKS

Come Back, Paul
I Go Out
Bubbles

THE SPEED OF DARKNESS

MURIEL RUKEYSER

THE SPEED OF DARKNESS

 RANDOM HOUSE · NEW YORK

ACKNOWLEDGMENTS

The author wishes to thank the editors and publishers of the following magazines, in which some of these poems first appeared: *Kenyon Review, The Nation, The Observer* (London), *Atlantic Monthly, Ikon, Liberation, Ladies' Home Journal, Saturday Review, American Judaism, Poetry* (Chicago), *New Directions, Annual, The New Yorker,* Macmillan, Unicorn Press, *Sarah Lawrence Journal, Poets for Peace,* War Resisters Calendar, *Chelsea, Ramparts, Evergreen Review.* The poem "Endless" appeared originally in *The New Yorker.* The poems "The Outer Banks" and "Delta Poems" appeared originally in *Poetry.*

"Delta Poems" was first read at Angry Arts Week; "Käthe Kollwitz" was first read at Syracuse University; "The Speed of Darkness" was first read at M.I.T.

The author wishes to thank the National Council on the Arts for a grant during the time of which many of these poems were written.

CONTENTS

*
*

    *
*

x

I CLUES

THE POEM AS MASK

ORPHEUS

When I wrote of the women in their dances and wildness,
    it was a mask,
on their mountain, god-hunting, singing, in orgy,
it was a mask; when I wrote of the god,
fragmented, exiled from himself, his life, the love gone
    down with song,
it was myself, split open, unable to speak, in exile from
    myself.

There is no mountain, there is no god, there is memory
of my torn life, myself split open in sleep, the rescued child
beside me among the doctors, and a word
of rescue from the great eyes.

No more masks! No more mythologies!

Now, for the first time, the god lifts his hand,
the fragments join in me with their own music.

WHAT DO I GIVE YOU?

What do I give you?   This memory
I cannot give you.   Force of a memory
I cannot give you : it rings my nerves among.
None of these songs
Are made in their images.
Seeds of all memory
Given me give I you
My own self.   Voice of my days.
Blessing;   the seed and pain,
Green of the praise of growth.
The sacred body of thirst.

THE TRANSGRESS

That summer midnight under her aurora
northern and still we passed the barrier.

Two make a curse, one giving, one accepting.
It takes two to break a curse

transformed at last in each other's eyes.

I sat on the naked bed of space,
all things becoming other than what they seem

in the night-waking, in the revelation
thundering on tabu after the broken

imperative, while the grotesque ancestors fade
with you breathing beside me through our dream:

bed of forbidden things finally known —
art from the symbol struck, living and made.

Branch lifted green from the dead shock of stone.

THE CONJUGATION OF THE PARAMECIUM

This has nothing
to do with
propagating

The species
is continued
as so many are
(among the smaller creatures)
by fission

(and this species
is very small
next in order to
the amoeba, the beginning one)

The paramecium
achieves, then,
immortality
by dividing

But when
the paramecium
desires renewal
strength   another joy
this is what
the paramecium does:

The paramecium
lies down beside
another
paramecium

Slowly   inexplicably
the exchange
takes place
in which
some bits
of the nucleus of each
are exchanged

for some bits
of the nucleus
of the other

This is called
the conjugation of the paramecium.

*
*

JUNK-HEAP AT MURANO

for Joby West

You told me : they all went in and saw the glass,
The tourists, and I with them, a busload of them,
    a boatload
Out from Venice. We saw the glass making.
Until I, longing for air — longing for something — walked
    outside
And found my way along the building and around.
Suddenly there the dazzle, all the colors, fireworks and
    jewels in a mound
Flashing from the heap of glass thrown away. Not quite
    perfect. Perhaps a little flawed. Chipped, perhaps.
        Here is one.
And handed me the blue.

I looked into your eyes
Who walked around Murano
And I saw far behind, the face of the child I carried out-
    doors that night.
You were four. You looked up into the great tree netting
    all of night
And saw fire-points in the tree, and asked, "Do birds eat
    stars?"

Behind your eyes the seasons, the times,
assemble; dazzle; are here.

*
*

CLUES

How will you catch these clues at the moment of waking
take them, make them yours?   Wake, do you,
and light the lamp of sharpest whitest beam
and write them down in the room of night on white —
night opening and opening white
paper under white light, write what streamed
from you in darkness
into you by dark?

Indian Baptiste saying, We painted our dreams.
We painted our dreams on our faces and bodies.
We took them into us by painting them on ourselves.

    When we saw the water mystery of the lake
after the bad dream, we painted the lines and masks,
when the bear wounded me, I painted for healing.
When we were told in our dreams, in the colors of day
red for earth, black for the opposite, rare green, white.
Yellow. When I dreamed of weeping and dreamed of sor-
row I painted my face with tears, with joy.
Our ghost paintings and our dreams of war.
The whole brow, the streak, the hands and sex, the breast.
The spot of white, one hand black, one hand red.
The morning star appearing over the hill.
We took our dreams into our selves.
We took our dreams into our bodies.

*
*

9

IN OUR TIME

In our period, they say there is free speech.
They say there is no penalty for poets,
There is no penalty for writing poems.
They say this.   This is the penalty.

DOUBLE DIALOGUE:

HOMAGE TO ROBERT FROST

In agony saying : "The last night of his life,
My son and I in the kitchen : At half-past one
He said, 'I have failed as a husband. Now my wife
Is ill again and suffering.' At two
He said, 'I have failed as a farmer, for the sun
Is never there, the rain is never there.'
At three he said, 'I have failed as a poet who
Has never not once found my listener.
There is no sense to my life.' But then he heard me out.
I argued point by point. Seemed to win. Won.
He spoke to me once more when I was done:
'Even in argument, father, I have lost.'
He went and shot himself. Now tell me this one thing:
Should I have let him win then? Was I wrong?"

To answer for the land for love for song
Arguing life for life even at your life's cost.

THE SIX CANONS

(after Binyon)

Seize structure.
Correspond with the real.
Fuse spirit and matter.
Know your own secrets.
Announce your soul in discovery.
Go toward the essence, the impulse of creation,
   where power comes in music from the sex,
   where power comes in music from the spirit,
   where sex and spirit are one self
   passing among
   and acting on all things
   and their relationships,
   moving the constellations of all things.

FORERUNNERS

Forerunners of images.
In morning, on the river-mouth,
I came to my waking
seeing carried in air
seaward, a ship.
Standing on stillness
before the bowsprit
the man of spirit
— lookout aloft, steersman at wheel, silence on water —
and the young graceful man holding the lily iron.
I dream of all harpooning and the sea.

Out of Seville, after Holy Week I heard the
story of the black carriage and a lordly woman.
Her four daughters, their skirts of black foam,
lace seethed about them; drawn by four horses,
reined in, their black threads in the coachman's hands.
Far ahead on invisible wire
a circus horse making his shapes on the air.
Between us forever enlarges Spain and the war.

Far in New Jersey, among split-level houses,
behind the concrete filling-station I found
a yellow building and the flags of prayer.
Two Tibetans in their saffron bowed, priests
of their robes, their banners, their powers.
Little Tibetan children playing stickball

*
*

on the black road.
Day conscious and unconscious.
Words on the air.
Before the great
images arrive, riderless horses.
Words on an uproar silent hour.
In our own time.

ORGY

There were three of them that night.
They wanted it to happen in the first woman's room.
The man called her; the phone rang high.
Then she put fresh lipstick on.
Pretty soon he rang the bell.
She dreamed, she dreamed, she dreamed.
She scarcely looked him in the face
But gently took him to his place.
And after that the bell, the bell.
They looked each other in the eyes,
A hot July it was that night,
And he then slow took off his tie,
And she then slow took off her scarf,
The second one took off her scarf,
And he then slow his heavy shoe,
And she then slow took off her shoe,
The other one took off her shoe,
He then took off his other shoe,
The second one, her other shoe,
A hot July it was that night.
And he then slow took off his belt,
And she then slow took off her belt,
The second one took off her belt . . .

THE OVERTHROW OF
ONE O'CLOCK AT NIGHT

is my concern.   That's this moment,
when I lean on my elbows out the windowsill
and feel the city among its time-zones, among its seas,
among its late night news, the pouring in
of everything meeting, wars, dreams, winter night.
Light in snowdrifts causing the young girls
lying awake to fall in love tonight
alone in bed; or the little children
half world over tonight rained on by fire — that's us —
calling on somebody — that's us — to come
and help them.
              Now I see at the boundary of darkness
extreme of moonlight.
                Alone.   All my hopes
scattered in people quarter world away
half world away, out of all hearing.
                    Tell myself:
Trust in experience.   And in the rhythms.
The deep rhythms of your experience.

AMONG GRASS

Lying here among grass, am I dead am I sleeping
amazed among silences   you touch me never
Here deep under, the small white moon
cries like a dime and do I hear?

The sun gone copper or I dissolve
no touch no touch   a tactless land
denies my death my fallen hand
silence runs down the riverbeds

One tall wind walks over my skin
                        breeze, memory
bears to my body (as the world fades)
                            going in
very late in the world's night to see roses opening
Remember, love, lying among roses.
Did we not lie among roses?

WHAT I SEE

Lie there, in sweat and dream, I do, and "there"
Is here, my bed, on which I dream
You, lying there, on yours, locked, pouring love,
While I tormented here see in my reins
You, perfectly at climax. And the lion strikes.
I want you with whatever obsessions come —
I wanted your obsession to be mine
But if it is that unknown half-suggested strange
Other figure locked in your climax, then
I here, I want you and the other, want your obsession, want
Whatever is locked into you now while I sweat and dream.

BELIEVING IN THOSE INEXORABLE LAWS

Believing in those inexorable laws
After long rebellion and long discipline
I am cut down to the moment in all my flaws
Creeping to the feet of my master the sun
On the sea-beach, tides beaten by the moon woman,
And will not think of you, but lie at my full length
Among the great breakers. I find the clear outwater
Shine crash speaking of truth behind the law.

The many-following waves turn into you.
I see in vision that northern bay : pines, villages,
And the flat water suddenly rears up
The high wave races against all edicts, taller,
Finally powerful. Water becomes your mouth,
And all laws all polarities your truth.

SONG : LOVE IN WHOSE RICH HONOR

Love
in whose rich honor
I stand looking from my window
over the starved trees of a dry September
Love
deep and so far forbidden
is bringing me
a gift
to claw at my skin
to break open my eyes
the gift longed for so long
The power
to write
out of the desperate ecstasy at last
death and madness

NIOBE NOW

Niobe
> wild
>> with unbelief
>>> at all
>>>> her ending
>>>>> turns to stone

Not gentle
> weeping
>> and souvenirs
>>> but hammering
>>>> honking
>>>>> agonies

Forty-nine tragic years
> are done
>> and the twentieth century
>>> not begun:

All tears,
> all tears,
>> all tears.

Water
> from her rock
>> is sprung
>>> and in this water
>>>> lives a seed

That must endure
> and grow
>> and shine

*
*

                        beasts, gardens
                                    at last rivers
A man
        to be born
                    to start again
                                to tear
                                    a woman
                                        from his side
And wake
            to start
                the world again.

SONG : THE STAR IN THE NETS OF HEAVEN

The star in the nets of heaven blazed past your breastbone,
Willing to shine among the nets of your growth,
The nets of your love,
The bonds of your dreams.

AIR

Flowers of air
with lilac defining air;
buildings of air
with walls defining air;
this May, people of air
advance along the street;
framed in their bodies, air,
their eyes speaking to me,
air in their mouths made
into live meanings.

GIFT

the child, the poems, the child, the poems, the journeys
    back and forth across our long country
        of opposites,
and through myself, through you, away from you, toward
    you, the dreams of madness and of an
        impossible complete time —
gift be forgiven.

CRIES FROM CHIAPAS

Hunger
    of mountains
            spoke
                from a tiger's throat.
Tiger-tooth peaks.
            The moon.
                    A thousand mists
turning.
            Desires of mountains
                    like the desires of women,
moon-drawn,
            distant,
                    clear black among
                            confusions of silver.
Women of Chiapas!
            Dream-borne
                    voices of women.
Splinters of mountains,
                    broken obsidian,
                            silver.
White tigers
        haunting
            your forehead here
                    sloped in shadow —
black hungers of women,
                    confusion
                            turning like tigers

And your voice —

I am
    almost asleep
        almost awake
            in your arms.

*
*

THE WAR COMES INTO MY ROOM

Knowing again
       that nothing
           has been spoken
              not now
                  not this night time
the broken singing
         as we move
             or of
               the endless war
                   our lives
that above all
         there is not said
              nothing
                  of this moment
in the poems
       our love
          in all the songs
             now I will
                live out
                  this moment
saying
    it
      in my breath
          to you
            across the air

DELTA POEMS

Among leaf-green
this morning, they
walk near water-blue,
near water-green
of the river-mouths
this boy   this girl
they die with their heads near each other,
their young mouths
*

A sharp glint out among the sea
These are lives coming out of their craft
Men who resemble. . . .
Sound is bursting the sun
Two dead bodies against the leaves
A young man and a girl
Their heads close together
No weapons, only grasses and waves
Lives, grasses
*

Something is flying through the high air over the
        river-mouth country,
Something higher than the look can go,
Higher than herons fly,
Higher than planes is it?
It is nothing now
But now it is sound beyond bigness
Turns into the hugeness : death. A leaf shakes on the sky.
*

*
*

Of the children in flames, of the grown man
his face burned to the bones, of the full woman
her body stopped from the nipples down, nursing
the live strong baby at her breast
I do not speak.

I am a woman
in a New York room
late in the twentieth century.

I am crying. I will write no more. —
Young man and girl walking along the sea,
among the leaves.

*

Fresh hot day among the river-mouths,
yellow-green leaves   green rivers running to sea.
A young man and a girl
go walking in the delta country
The war has lasted their entire lifetime.
They look at each other with their mouths.
They look at each other with their whole bodies.
A glint as of bright fire, metal over the sea-waters.

*

A girl has died upon green leaves,
a young man has died against the sky.
A girl is walking printed against green leaves,
A young man walks printed upon the sky.

*

I remember you. We walked near the harbor.
You a young man believing in the future of summer,

*
*

in yellow, in green, in touch, in entering,
in the night-sky, in the gifts of this effort.
He believes in January,
he believes in the pulses beating along his body,
he believes in her young year.

I walk near the rivers.

*

They are walking again at the edge of waters.
They are killed again near the lives, near the waves.
They are walking, their heads are close together,
their mouths are close as they die.
A girl and a young man walk near the water.

*
*

SPIRALS AND FUGUES

Spirals and fugues, the power most like music
Turneth all worlds to meaning
And meaning to matter, all continually,
And sweeps in the sacred motion,
Spirals and fugues its lifetime,
To move my life to yours,
   and all women and men and the children in their light,
The little stone in the middle of the road, its veins and
    patience,
Moving the constellations of all things.

*
*

ANEMONE

My eyes are closing, my eyes are opening.
You are looking into me with your waking look.

My mouth is closing, my mouth is opening.
You are waiting with your red promises.

My sex is closing, my sex is opening.
You are singing and offering : the way in.

My life is closing, my life is opening.
You are here.

FIGHTING FOR ROSES

After the last freeze, in easy air,
Once the danger is past, we cut them back severely;
Pruning the weakest hardest, pruning for size'
Of flower, we deprived will not deprive the sturdy.
The new shoots are preserved, the future bush
Cut down to a couple of young dormant buds.

But the early sun of April does not burn our lives :
Light straight and fiery brings back the enemies.
Claw, jaw, and crawler, all those that devour.
We work with smoke against the robber blights,
With copper against rust; the season fights itself
In deep strong rich loam under swarm attacks.

Head hidden from the wind, the power of form
Rises among these brightnesses, thorned and blowing.
Where they glow on the earth, water-drops tremble on
    them.
Soon we must cut them back, against damage of storms.
But those days gave us flower budded on flower,
A moment of light achieved, deep in the air of roses.

FOR MY SON

You come from poets, kings, bankrupts, preachers,
    attempted bankrupts, builders of cities, salesmen,
the great rabbis, the kings of Ireland, failed drygoods
    storekeepers, beautiful women of the songs,
great horsemen, tyrannical fathers at the shore of ocean,
    the western mothers looking west beyond from their
        windows,
the families escaping over the sea hurriedly and by night —
the roundtowers of the Celtic violet sunset,
the diseased, the radiant, fliers, men thrown out of town,
    the man bribed by his cousins to stay out of town,
        teachers, the cantor on Friday evening, the lurid
           newspapers,
strong women gracefully holding relationship, the Jewish
    girl going to parochial school, the boys racing their
        iceboats on the Lakes,
the woman still before the diamond in the velvet window,
    saying "Wonder of nature."
Like all men,
you come from singers, the ghettoes, the famines, wars and
    refusal of wars, men who built villages
that grew to our solar cities, students, revolutionists, the
    pouring of buildings, the market newspapers,
a poor tailor in a darkening room,
a wilderness man, the hero of mines, the astronomer, a
    white-faced woman hour on hour teaching piano and
        her crippled wrist,

*
*

like all men,
you have not seen your father's face
but he is known to you forever in song, the coast of the
skies, in dream, wherever you find man playing his
part as father, father among our light, among our
darkness,
and in your self made whole, whole with yourself and
whole with others,
the stars your ancestors.

POEM

I lived in the first century of world wars.
Most mornings I would be more or less insane,
The newspapers would arrive with their careless stories,
The news would pour out of various devices
Interrupted by attempts to sell products to the unseen.
I would call my friends on other devices;
They would be more or less mad for similar reasons.
Slowly I would get to pen and paper,
Make my poems for others unseen and unborn.
In the day I would be reminded of those men and women
Brave, setting up signals across vast distances,
Considering a nameless way of living, of almost
     unimagined values.
As the lights darkened, as the lights of night brightened,
We would try to imagine them, try to find each other.
To construct peace, to make love, to reconcile
Waking with sleeping, ourselves with each other,
Ourselves with ourselves. We would try by any means
To reach the limits of ourselves, to reach beyond ourselves,
To let go the means, to wake.

  I lived in the first century of these wars.

THE POWER OF SUICIDE

The potflower on the windowsill says to me
In words that are green-edged red leaves :
Flower   flower   flower   flower
Today for the sake of all the dead   Burst into flower.

(1963)

THE SEEMING

for Helen Lynd

Between the illuminations of great mornings
there comes the dailiness of doing and being
and the hand as it makes as it brightens   burnishes
the surfaces   seemings   mirrors of the world

We do not know the springs of these colored and loving
acts   or what triggers birth   what sleep is
but name them as we name bird-wakened morning
having our verbs of the world
to which all action seems
to resolve, being

to go, to grow, to flow, to shine, to sound, to glow,
to give and to take, to bind and to separate,
to injure   and to defend

we do not even   not even know why we wake

but some of us showing the others
a kind of welcoming
bringing a form to morning
as a woman who recognizes
may offer us the moment and the names
turning all shame into a declaration
immediately to be followed by
an act of truth

*
*

39

until all seemings are

                          illumination

we see in a man a theme
a dream taking over
or in this woman going today who has shown us
fear, and form, and storm turned into light
the dailiness of our being and doing
morning and every time the way to naming
and we see more now coming into being

see in her goings as in her arrivings
the opening of a door

*
*

40

SONG FROM *PUCK FAIR*

Torrent that rushes down
Knocknadober,
Make the channel deeper
Where I ferry home.

Winds go west over
Left-handed Reaper
Mountain that gathered me
Out of my old shame—

Your white beard streaming,
Puck of summertime,
At last gave me
My woman's name.

NOT YET

A time of destruction. Of the most rigid powers in ascen-
    dance.
Secret plots against them, open work against them in
    round buildings.
All fail. Any work for fluency, for freedom, fails.
Battles. The wiping out of cities full of people.
Long tracts of devastation.

In one city : a scene of refugees, each allowed to take
a suitcase of bedding, blankets, no more. An old man, a
    professor.
He has hidden a few books and two small statues in a
    blanket
and packed his case. He comes in his turn to the examining
    desk.
He struggles about the lie he needs to tell. He lies, he de-
    clares nothing.
Even after the lie, the suitcase is thrown over the cliff
where all the statues lie broken, the books, pictures, the
    records.

Long landscapes of devastation. Color modulated between
sparse rigid monuments. Long orange landscapes
shifting to yellow-orange to show a generation.
Long passage of time to yellow. Only these elite,
their army tread on yellow terrain. Their schools. Their
    children.

*
*

A tradition of rigor, hatred and doom is now
— generations after — the only sole tradition.
I am looking at the times and time as at a dream.
As at the recurrent dream of a locked room.
I think of the solution of the sealed room mystery
of the chicken and the egg, in which the chicken
feeds on his cell, grows strong on the sealed room
and finally
        in strength
               eating his prison
pierces the shell.
          How can this room change state?
I see its sky, its children. I cannot imagine.

I look at the young faces of the children
in this tradition, far down the colors of the years.
They are still repeating their shut slogans
with "war" substituted for freedom. But their faces glow.
The children are marvelous, singing among the wars.
They have needed the meanings, and their faces show
this : the solution.
         The words have taken on
all their forbidden meanings. The words mean their op-
    posites.
They must, they are needed.

Children's faces, lit, unlit,
the face of a child.

  *
 *

43

LANDSCAPE WITH WAVE APPROACHING

I

All of the people of the play were there,
swam in the mile-long wave, among cliff-flowers
were pierced, hung and remembered a sunlit year.

II

By day white moths, the nightlong meteors
flying like snow among the flowery trees —
hissing like prophecy above those seas.

III

The city of the past. The past as a city
and all the people in it, your childhood faces,
their dances, their words developing, their hands.

IV

The fertile season ending in a glitter;
blight of the forest, orange, burning the trees away,
the checkered light. Full length on naked sand.

V

All of the people of the play were there,
smiling, telling their truths, coming to crisis.
This water, this water, this water. These rocks, this pierc-
    ing sea.

*
*

VI

Flower of time, and a plague of white trilling in sunlight,
the season advancing on the people of the play,
the scars on the mountains and the body of fire.

Carmel, California

SEGRE SONG

Your song where you lie long dead on the shore of a Span-
    ish river —
your song moves under the earth and through time,
    through air —
your song I sing to the sun as we move
and to the cities
sing to the mimosa
sing to the moon over my face

BUNK JOHNSON BLOWING

in memory of Leadbelly
and his house on 59th Street

They found him in the fields and called him back to music.
Can't, he said, my teeth are gone.   They bought him
    teeth.

Bunk Johnson's trumpet on a California
early May evening, calling me to
breath of . . .
up those stairs . . .
calling me to
look into
the face of that
trumpet
experience
and past it
his eyes

Jim and Rita beside me. We drank it. Jim had just come
    back
from Sacramento the houses made of piano boxes the bar
    without
a sign and the Mexicans drinking we drank that trumpet
    music
and drank that black park moonlit beneath the willow
    trees,

*
*

Bunk Johnson blowing all night out of that full moon.
Two-towered church. Rita listening to it, all night
music! said, I'm supposed to, despise them.
Tears streaming down her face. Said, don't tell my ancestors.

We three slid down that San Francisco hill.

CANNIBAL BRATUSCHA

Have you heard about Mr. Bratuscha?
He led an orderly life
With a splendid twelve-year-old daughter,
A young and passionate wife —
  Bratuscha, the one they call Cannibal.

Spring evening on Wednesday,
The sky is years ago;
The girl has been missing since Monday,
Why don't the birches blow?
  And where's their daughter?

Nine miles to the next village
Deep in the forested past —
Wheatland, marshland, daisies
And a gold slender ghost.
  It's very difficult to keep them safe.

She hasn't been seen and its Thursday.
Down by the river, raped?
Under the birches, murdered?
Don't let the fiend escape,
  First, we'll track him down and catch him.

The river glittering in sunlight,
The woods almost black — and she
Was always a darling, the blonde young daughter,

*
*

Gone gone vanished away.
   They say Bratuscha is ready to talk.

O God he has told the whole story;
Everything; he has said
That he killed his golden daughter
He ate her, he said it!
   Eaten by the cannibal, Cannibal Bratuscha.

Down at the church her mother
In the confession booth —
She has supported his story,
She has told the priest the truth;
   Horror, and now the villagers gather.

They are ready to lynch Bratuscha,
Pounding at his door —
Over the outcries of the good people
Hear the cannibal roar —
   He will hold out, bar the doorway, fight to the death.

But who is this coming, whose shadow
Runs down the river road?
She is coming, she is running, she is
Alive and abroad —
   She is here, she is well, she was in the next village.

The roaring dreams of her father :
He believed all he confessed —
And the mother was threatened with hellfire

   *
 *

By the village priest
  If she didn't tell everything, back up what Bratuscha
    said.

This all took place some time ago
Before all villages joined —
When there were separate, uncivilized people,
Only the birds, only the river, only dreams and the wind.
  She had just gone off for a few days, with a friend.

But O God the little Bratuscha girl
What will become of her?
Her mother is guilt suggestion panic
Her father of dreams, a murderer
  And in waking and in fantasy and now and forever.

Who will help her and you and me and all those
Children of the assumption of guilt
And the roaring fantasy of nightmare
The bomb the loathing all dreams spilt
  Upon this moment and the future and all unborn chil-
    dren.

We must go deep go deep in our lives and our dreams —
Remember Cannibal Bratuscha his wife and his young
    child
And preserve our own ideas of guilt
Of innocence and of the blessed wild
  To live out our own lives to make our own freedom to
    make the world.

*

WHAT HAVE YOU BROUGHT
HOME FROM THE WARS?

What have you brought
home from the wars, father?
Scars.
We fought far overseas; we knew
the victory must
be at home.
But here I see
only a trial by time
of those
who know.
The public men all shout : Come bomb,
come burn
our hate.
I do not
want it shot;
I want it solved.
This is the word
the dead men said.
They said peace.
I saw in the hot light
of our century
each face killed.

ONE MONTH

for Dorothy Lear

All this time
you were dead and I did not know
I was learning to speak
and speaking to you
and you were not there
I was seeing you
tall, walking the corridor
of that tall shining building
I was learning to walk
and walking to you
and it was not true
you were still living still lying still
it was not true
that you were giving me a rose
telling me stories
pouring a wine-story, there were bubbles in it
all this time
I was remembering untrue
speaking untrue, seeing a lie.

It is true.

SILENCE OF VOLCANOES

I

The mountains and the shadows move away
Under their snows to show an immense scene:
A field of cathedrals. Green domes eye-green,
Domes the color of trumpets. Obliterated rose
And impure copper. Vaults are pale shoulders.
Grass-haired and deformed,
The dome-capped pyramid to the god of the air.
A white dome under these volcanoes.
This is the field that glittered in massacre,
Time is boiling with domes.

II

A woman has been begging for ninety-seven years.
The singing of her words against shadows of gold.
I see her lean her face against this scene.
The domes dissolve. All her unfallen tears.
I remember a room for sale in a picture
Torn as this landscape
Obsessed by a single thing.

III

A hall at the National Pawnshop crowded with unsold
 bureaus.
In sharp paint at the end of a blind aisle
Red-robed and listening, the saint looks at the Sign.

*
*

Books fold him in, strict black-and-white tile
Lead to a sleeping garden where his lion,
The guardian, lies in a silence of volcanoes.
Hung in that air, there pierces his leaning soul
The cheap tin trumpet that is the voice of God.

Mexico

WHAT THEY SAID

:   After I am dead, darling,
      my seventeen senses gone,
I shall love you as you wish,
    no sex, no mouth, but bone —
    in the way you long for now,
with my soul alone.

:   When we are neither woman nor man
      but bleached to skeleton —
when you have changed, my darling,
    and all your senses gone,
    it is not me that you will love:
you will love everyone.

A LITTLE STONE IN THE MIDDLE
OF THE ROAD, IN FLORIDA

My son as a child saying
God
is anything, even a little stone in the middle of the road,
    in Florida.
Yesterday
Nancy, my friend, after long illness:
You know what can lift me up, take me right out of
    despair?
No, what?
Anything.

THE BLUE FLOWER

for Frances C. Wickes
on her ninetieth birthday,
August 28, 1965

Stroke by stroke, in the country of the fragile
stroke by stroke, each act a season
speaking the years of making
this flower
shining over the fears
over the cities
and the camps of death.
Shines from a field
of eighty-seven years,
the young child and the dream.

In my city of stone,
water and light
I saw the blue flower
held still, and flying —
never seen by me
but in your words given;
fragile, mortal
that endures.

By turns flying and still.
"Angkor Vat, a gray stone city
but the flight of kingfishers

all day enlivened it" —
a blue flash given to us, past stone and time.

Blaze of mortality
piercing, tense
the structure of a dream
speaking and fragile,
momentary,
for now
and ever and all
your blue flower.

*
*

WOMAN AS MARKET

—FORGETTING AND REMEMBERING—

What was it? What was it?
Flashing beside me, lightning in daylight at the orange
    stand?
Along the ranks of eggs, beside the loaves of dark and
    light?
In a moment of morning, providing:
the moment of the eggplant?
            the lemons? the fresh eggs?
with their bright curves and curves of shadow?
the reds, the yellows, all the calling boxes.
What did those forms say? What words have I forgotten?
what spoke to me from the day?
God in the cloud? my life in my forgetting?
I have forgotten what it was
that I have been trying to remember

*
*

WORD OF MOUTH

I — THE RETURN

Westward from Sète
                    as I went long before
along my life
              as I went
                        wave by wave —
the long words of the sea
                          the orange rooftop tiles
back to the boundary
                     where I had been before.

Spain.
           Sex of cactus and of cypresses,
Tile-orange, green;   olive;   black.   The sea.
One man.   Beethoven radio.   War.
Threat of all life.   Within my belief's body.
Within my morning, music.   High colored mountain
along the seacoast
                   where the swallows fly.

Prolonged
beyond your cries and your cities.

Note:
The country is the Catalan border of France and Spain. The two
times are July, 1936, the beginning of the war, and the time of
my return to the border in 1963.

*
*

61

Along my life and death backward toward that morning
when all things fell open and I went into Spain.

One man.   Sardana music.   This frontier.
Where I now come again.

I stop.

I do not pass.

Wave under wave
               like the divisive South
afire in the country of my birth.

A moment of glass.   All down the coast I face
as far as vision, blue, memory of blue.

Seen now.   Why do I not go in?   I stand.
I cannot pass.   History, destroyed music.

I need to go into.
                In a dream I have seen
Spain, *sleeping children:*

before me:

as I drive

as I go
        (I need to go into

this country
of love and)

wave after wave

they lie

in a deep forest.
                    As the driving light
touches them
                    (I need this country
                                        of love and death)
they begin to rouse.
                    They wake.

II — WORD OF MOUTH

Speeding back from the border.

A rock came spinning up
cast from the wheels of a car.

Crackled the windshield glass.
Glitter before my eyes like a man made of snow
lying over the hood, blind white except for glints
an inch of sight where Languedoc shines through.

You on my one side, you on the other!
What I have is dazzle.   My son; my friend;
tell me this side and tell me that side,
news of the road near Agde.

Word from this side, word from the tree-side —
Spain at our back : agony : before me, glitter,

today
blinding my eyes, blind diamonds, one clear wound.

Something is flying out of the sky behind me.
Turning, stirring of dream, something is speeding,
something is overtaking.

Stirrings in prisons, on beds, the mouths of the young,
resist, dance, love.   It drives through the back of my
    head,
through my eyes and breasts and mouth.

*
*

I know a harvest : mass in the wine country.
A lifetime after, and still alive.

Something out of Spain, into the general light!
I drive blind white, trusting news of this side,
news of that side, all the time the line of the poem:
Amor, pena, desig, somni, dolor.
The grapes have become wine by the hand of man.
Sea risen from the sea, a bearded king.

The seaward cemetery risen from the sea
like a woman rising.
                    Amor.
                              Phases of sun.
The wine declared god by the hand of man.
Pena.
          A rumor given me by this side and that side.
We drive in brilliant glitter, in jungle night, in distant war,
in all our cities, in a word, overtaking.
                              Desig.

A cry received, gone past me into all men,
speaking, into all women.
                    A man goes into the sea,
bearded fire and all things rise from this blaze of eyes,
living, it speaks, driving forth from Spain,
                              somni, dolor,

These cliffs, these years.   Do we drive into light?
Driven, live, overtaken?

Amor, pena, desig.

Note:
The line is from a Catalan poem in *Cantilena* by Joseph Sebastien Pons. *Love, agony, desire, dream, suffering.*

ENDLESS

Under the tall black sky you look out of your body
lit by a white flare of the time between us
your body with its touch its weight   smelling of new
    wood
as on the day the news of battle reached us
falls beside the endless river
flowing to the endless sea
whose waves come to this shore a world away.

Your body of new wood your eyes alive barkbrown of tree-
    trunks
the leaves and flowers of trees   stars all caught in crowns
    of trees
your life gone down, broken into endless earth
no longer a world away but under my feet and everywhere
I look down at the one earth under me,
through to you and all the fallen
the broken and their children born and unborn
of the endless war.

11 GAMES

THE BACKSIDE OF THE ACADEMY

Five brick panels, three small windows, six lions' heads
    with rings in their mouths, five pairs of closed bronze
        doors—
the shut wall with the words carved across its head
ART REMAINS THE ONE WAY POSSIBLE OF SPEAK-
    ING TRUTH.—
On this May morning, light swimming in this street, the
    children running,
on the church beside the Academy the lines are flying
of little yellow-and-white plastic flags flapping in the light;
and on the great shut wall, the words are carved across:
WE ARE YOUNG AND WE ARE FRIENDS OF
    TIME.—
Below that, a light blue asterisk in chalk
and in white chalk, Hector, Joey, Lynn, Rudolfo.
A little up the street, a woman shakes a small dark boy,
she shouts What's wrong with you, ringing that bell!
In the street of rape and singing, poems, small robberies,
carved in an oblong panel of the stone:
CONSCIOUS UTTERANCE OF THOUGHT BY
    SPEECH OR ACTION
TO ANY END IS ART.—
On the lowest reach of the walls are chalked the words:
    Jack is a object,
Walter and Trina, Goo Goo, I love Trina,
and further along Viva Fidel now altered to Muera Fidel.
A deep blue marble is lodged against the curb.

*
*

A phone booth on one corner; on the other, the big mesh
    basket for trash.
Beyond them, the little park is always locked. For the two
    soldier brothers.
and past that goes on an eternal football game
which sometimes, as on this day in May, transforms to
    stickball
as, for one day in May,
five pairs of closed bronze doors will open
and the Academy of writers, sculptors, painters, com-
    posers, their guests and publishers will all roll in and
the wave of organ music come rolling out into
The street where light now blows and papers and little
        children and words, some breezes of Spanish blow
        and many colors of people.
A watch cap lies fallen against a cellophane which used to
    hold pistachio nuts
and here before me, on my street,
five brick panels, three small windows, six lions' heads with
    rings in their mouths, five pairs of closed bronze doors,
light flooding the street I live and write in; and across the
    river the one word FREE against the ferris wheel and
        the roller coaster,
and here, painted upon the stones, Chino, Bobby, Joey,
    Fatmoma, Willy, Holy of God
and also Margaret is a shit and also fuck and shit;
far up, invisible at the side of the building:
WITHOUT VISION THE PEO
and on the other side, the church side,

*
*

where shadows of trees and branches, this day in May, are
    printed balanced on the church wall,
in-focus trunks and softened-focus branches
below the roof where the two structures stand,
bell and cross, antenna and weathervane,
I can see past the church the words of an ending line:
IVE BY BREAD ALONE.

MOUNTAIN : ONE FROM BRYANT

Wildflowers withering with the same death.
Grave a slope, threw she long shadows,
Mountains o'erlooking earth, affect and places
High.   On God that time, the elder worshipper,
Deemed spirit, made here a tribe of offering,
Bear and wolf of skins shaggy, maze of ears
And garlands lay.   Mother, my dreams, night and
Mockings like friends, pastimes hate I
And business accursed upon me glares;
The life of the sick is sorrow, guilt, and love.
Eye her then, vain in might, simple as heart.
Heaven props earth with columns; mountains raise
Distances, blue in hills, upward swell fields.
Man has ages for soil, mining himself
To paradise.   The scene murmurs.   Struggle with
    winds,
Hear depth dizzy the ear, a thunderbolt of whiteness.

Note:
This is a poem of William Cullen Bryant's that is run backward
("What?" said Denise Levertov. "You mean 'Foul Water' instead
of 'Waterfowl'?" "Exactly," I said.) The poem is "Monument
Mountain," out of which I took key words and phrases and ran
the film backward.

*
*

Centuries of growth, darkness of capitals,
Pinnacles and trees shaggy and wild.
North to the drowned!   and nations separate the world.
Shriek eagle in your torrent solitude.
Glens of secret, down into forest-tops,
Beneath a wide-spread earth; majesty and beauty
Fail.   Foot mountains.   Though rocky our ascent,
Face nature in harmony, lovely, and face it!   wild.

THE FLYING RED HORSE

On all the streetcorners the children are standing,
They ask What can it mean?
The grownups answer   A flying red horse
Signifies gasoline.

The man at the Planetarium,
Pointing beyond the sky,
Is not going to say that Pegasus
Means poetry.

Some of our people feel like death,
And some feel rather worse.
His energy, in this night of lies,
Flies right against the curse.

What's *red?*   What is the *flying horse?*
They swear they do not know,
But just the same, and every night,
All the streetcorners glow.

Even the Pentagon, even the senators,
Even the President sitting on his arse —
Never mind — over all cities
The flying red horse.

*
*

III THE OUTER BANKS

THE OUTER BANKS

I

Horizon of islands shifting
Sea-light flame on my voice
                     burn in me
                          Light
flows from the water from sands   islands of this horizon
The sea comes toward me across the sea.   The sand
moves over the sand in waves
between the guardians of this landscape
the great commemorative statue on one hand
    — the first flight of man, outside of dream,
          seen as stone wing and stainless steel —
and at the other hand
    banded black-and-white, climbing
the spiral lighthouse.

Note:
This country, the Outer Banks of North Carolina, is a strong country of imagination: Raleigh's first settlements, in which Thomas Hariot the scientist served a year in the New World, were here; the Wright Brothers flew from here; Hart Crane's "Hatteras" is set among these sand-bars, these waters. Several journeys here, the last one for the sake of the traces of Thomas Hariot (toward a biography I am writing) led me to this poem. The *Tiger,* in the last part of the poem, is one of the ships sent out by Raleigh. The quotations are from Selma, Alabama, in 1965. The truncated wing is a monument to the Wright Brothers. The spiral lighthouse is Hatteras light.

*
*

II

Flood over ocean,
avalanche on the flat beach. Pouring.
Indians holding branches up, to
placate the tempest,
the one-legged twisting god that is
a standing wind.
Rays are branching from all things:
great serpent, great plume, constellation:
sands from which colors and light pass,
the lives of plants.   Animals.   Men.
A man and a woman reach for each other.

III

Wave of the sea.

IV

Sands have washed, sea has flown over us.
Between the two guardians, spiral, truncated wing,
history and these wild birds
Bird-voiced discoverers : Hariot,   Hart Crane,
the brothers who watched gulls.
"No bird soars in a calm,"   said Wilbur Wright.
Dragon of the winds forms over me.
Your dance, goddesses in your circle
sea-wreath, whirling of the event
behind me on land as deep in our own lives
we begin to know the movement to come.

*
*

Sunken, drowned spirals,
hurricane-dance.

V

Shifting of islands on this horizon.
The cycle of changes in the Book of Changes.
Two islands making an open female line
That powerful long straight bar a male island.
The building of the surf
constructing immensities
between the pale flat Sound
and ocean ever
birds as before earthquake
winds fly from all origins
the length of this wave goes from the great wing
down coast, the barrier beach in all its miles
road of the sun and the moon to
a spiral lighthouse
to the depth turbulence
lifts up its wave like cities
the ocean in the air
spills down the world.

VI

A man is walking toward me across the water.
From far out, the flat waters of the Sound,
he walks pulling his small boat

In the shoal water.

*
*

A man who is white and has been fishing.
Walks steadily upon the light of day
Coming closer to me where I stand
looking into the sun and the blaze inner water.
Clear factual surface over which he pulls
a boat over a closing quarter-mile.

VII

Speak to it, says the light.
Speak to it music,
voices of the sea and human throats.
Origins of spirals,
the ballad and original sweet grape
dark on the vines near Hatteras,
tendrils of those vines, whose spiral tower
now rears its light, accompanying
all my voices.

VIII

He walks toward me.   A black man in the sun.
He now is a black man speaking to my heart
crisis of darkness in this century
of moments of this speech.

The boat is slowly nearer drawn, this man.

The zigzag power coming straight, in stones,
     in arcs, metal, crystal, the spiral
in sacred wet

*
*
82

                    schematic elements of
cities, music, arrangement
spin these stones of home
                              under the sea
return to the stations of the stars
and the sea, speaking across its lives.

IX

A man who is bones is close to me
drawing a boat of bones
the sun behind him
is another color of fire,
the sea behind me
rears its flame.

A man whose body flames and tapers in flame
twisted tines of remembrance that dissolve
a pitchfork of the land worn thin
flame up and dissolve again
                         draw   small   boat

Nets of the stars at sunset over us.
This draws me home to the home of the wild birds
long-throated birds of this passage.
This is the edge of experience, *grenzen der seele*
where those on the verge of human understanding
the borderline people stand on the shifting islands
among the drowned stars and the tempest.
"Everyman's mind, like the dumbest,

*
*
83

claws at his own furthest limits of knowing the world,"
a man in a locked room said.

Open to the sky
I stand before this boat that looks at me.
The man's flames are arms and legs.
Body, eyes, head, stars, sands look at me.

I walk out into the shoal water
and throw my leg over the wall of the boat.

X

At one shock, speechlessness.
I am in the bow, on the short thwart.
He is standing before me amidships, rowing forward
like my old northern sea-captain in his dory.
All things have spun.
The words gone,
I facing sternwards, looking at the gate
between the barrier islands.   As he rows.
Sand islands shifting and the last of land
a pale and open line   horizon
sea.

With whose face did he look at me?
What did I say?   or did I say?
in speechlessness
move to the change.
These strokes provide the music,

*
*

and the accused boy on land today saying
What did I say?   or did I say?
The dream on land last night built this the boat of death
but in the suffering of the light
moving across the sea
do we in our moving
move toward life or death

XI

Hurricane, skullface, the sky's size
winds streaming through his teeth
doing the madman's twist

and not a beach not flooded

nevertheless, here
stability of light
my other silence
and at my left hand and at my right hand
no longer wing and lighthouse
no longer the guardians.
They are in me, in my speechless
life of barrier beach.
As it lies open
to the night, out there.

Now seeing my death before me
starting again, among the drowned men,
desperate men, unprotected discoverers,

*
*

and the man before me
here.
Stroke by stroke drawing us.
Out there? Father of rhythms,
deep wave, mother.
There is no *out there*.
All is open.
Open water. Open I.

XII

The wreck of the *Tiger*, the early pirate, the blood-clam's
    ark, the tern's acute eye, all buried mathematical
        instruments, castaways, pelicans, drowned five-
            strand pearl necklaces, hopes of livelihood,
                hopes of grace,
walls of houses, sepia sea-fences, the writhen octopus and
    those tall masts and sails,
marked hulls of ships and last month's plane, dipping his
    salute to the stone wing of dream,
turbulence, Diamond Shoals, the dark young living peo-
    ple:
"Sing one more song and you are under arrest."
"Sing another song."
Women, ships, lost voices.
Whatever has dissolved into our waves.
I a lost voice
moving, calling you
on the edge of the moment that is now the center.
From the open sea.

   *
*
86

IV *LIVES*

AKIBA

THE WAY OUT

The night is covered with signs. The body and face of man,
with signs, and his journeys.   Where the rock is split
and speaks to the water;   the flame speaks to the cloud;
the red splatter, abstraction, on the door
speaks to the angel and the constellations.
The grains of sand on the sea-floor speak at last to the
    noon.
And the loud hammering of the land behind
speaks ringing up the bones of our thighs, the hoofs,
we hear the hoofs over the seethe of the sea.

Note:
These two "Lives" are part of a sequence. Akiba is the Jewish
shepherd-scholar of the first and second century, identified with
the Song of Songs and with the insurrection against Hadrian's
Rome, led in A.D. 132 by Bar Cochba (Son of the Star). After
this lightning war, Jerusalem captured, the Romans driven out of
the south, Rome increased its military machine; by 135, the last
defenses fell, Bar Cochba was killed, Akiba was tortured to death
at the command of his friend, the Roman Rufus, and a harrow
was drawn over the ground where Jerusalem had stood, leaving
only a corner of wall. The story in my mother's family is that we
are descended from Akiba—unverifiable, but a great gift to a
child.

The other "Lives," beside that of Käthe Kollwitz, the German
artist, are Charles Ives, Ryder, John Jay Chapman, Ann Burlak,
Willard Gibbs, Lord Timothy Dexter (all in *Waterlily Fire*).
To come are Franz Boas and Bessie Smith.

All night down the centuries, have heard, music of pas-
    sage.

Music of one child carried into the desert;
firstborn forbidden by law of the pyramid.
Drawn through the water with the water-drawn people
led by the water-drawn man to the smoke mountain.
The voice of the world speaking, the world covered by
    signs,
the burning, the loving, the speaking, the opening.
Strong throat of sound from the smoking mountain.
Still flame, the spoken singing of a young child.
The meaning beginning to move, which is the song.

Music of those who have walked out of slavery.

Into that journey where all things speak to all things
refusing to accept the curse, and taking
for signs the signs of all things, the world, the body
which is part of the soul, and speaks to the world,
all creation being created in one image, creation.
This is not the past walking into the future,
the walk is painful, into the present, the dance
not visible as dance until much later.
These dancers are discoverers of God.

We knew we had all crossed over when we heard the song.

Out of a life of building lack on lack:
the slaves refusing slavery, escaping into faith:

    *
  *

an army who came to the ocean: the walkers
who walked through the opposites, from I to opened Thou,
city and cleave of the sea. Those at flaming Nauvoo,
the ice on the great river: the escaping Negroes,
swamp and wild city: the shivering children of Paris
and the glass black hearses; those on the Long March:
all those who together are the frontier, forehead of man.

Where the wilderness enters, the world, the song of the
   world.

Akiba rescued, secretly, in the clothes of death
by his disciples carried from Jerusalem
in blackness journeying to find his journey
to whatever he was loving with his life.
The wilderness journey through which we move
under the whirlwind truth into the new,
the only accurate. A cluster of lights at night:
faces before the pillar of fire. A child watching
while the sea breaks open. This night. The way in.

Barbarian music, a new song.

Acknowledging opened water, possibility:
open like a woman to this meaning.
In a time of building statues of the stars,
valuing certain partial ferocious skills
while past us the chill and immense wilderness
spreads its one-color wings until we know
rock, water, flame, cloud, or the floor of the sea,

*
*

the world is a sign, a way of speaking. To find.
What shall we find? Energies, rhythms, journey.

Ways to discover. The song of the way in.

For THE SONG OF SONGS

However the voices rise
They are the shepherd, the king,
The woman; dreams,
Holy desire.

Whether the voices
Be many the dance around
Or body led by one body
Whose bed is green,

I defend the desire
Lightning and poetry
Alone in the dark city
Or breast to breast.

Champion of light I am
The wounded holy light,
The woman in her dreams
And the man answering.

*
*

You who answer their dreams
Are the ruler of wine
Emperor of clouds
And the riches of men.

This song
Is the creation
The day of this song
The day of the birth of the world.

Whether a thousand years
Forget this woman, this king,
Whether two thousand years
Forget the shepherd of dreams.

If none remember
Who is lover, who the beloved,
Whether the poet be
Woman or man,

The desire will make
A way through the wilderness
The leopard mountains
And the lips of the sleepers.

Holy way of desire,
King, lion, the mouth of the poet,
The woman who dreams
And the answerer of dreams.

*
*

In these delights
Is eternity of seed,
The verge of life,
Body of dreaming.

THE BONDS

In the wine country, poverty, they drink no wine —
In the endless night of love he lies, apart from love —
In the landscape of the Word he stares, he has no word.

He hates and hungers for his immense need.

He is young. This is a shepherd who rages at learning,
Having no words. Looks past green grass and sees a
          woman.
She, Rachel, who is come to recognize.
In the huge wordless shepherd she finds Akiba.

To find the burning Word. To learn to speak.

The body of Rachel says, the marriage says,
The eyes of Rachel say, and water upon rock
Cutting its groove all year says All things learn.
Me learns with his new son whose eyes are wine.

To sing continually, to find the word.

        *
      *

94

He comes to teaching, greater than the deed
Because it begets the deed, he comes to the stone
Of long ordeal, and suddenly knows the brook
Offering water, the citron fragrance, the light of candles.

All given, and always the giver loses nothing.

In giving, praising, we move beneath clouds of honor,
In giving, in praise, we take gifts that are given,
The spark from one to the other leaping, a bond
Of light, and we come to recognize the rock;

We are the rock acknowledging water, and water
Fire, and woman man, all brought through wilderness;
And Rachel finding in the wordless shepherd
Akiba who can now come to his power and speak:
The need to give having found the need to become:

More than the calf wants to suck, the cow wants to give
    such.

AKIBA MARTYR

When his death confronted him, it had the face of his
    friend
Rufus the Roman general with his claws of pain,
His executioner. This was an old man under iron rakes
Tearing through to the bone. He made no cry.

*
*

After the failure of all missions. At ninety, going
To Hadrian in Egypt, the silver-helmed,
Named for a sea. To intercede. Do not build in the rebuilt
   Temple
Your statue, do not make it a shrine to you.
Antinous smiling. Interpreters. This is an old man, plead-
   ing.
Incense of fans. The emperor does not understand.

He accepts his harvest, failures. He accepts faithlessness,
Madness of friends, a failed life; and now the face of storm.

Does the old man during uprising speak for compromise?
In all but the last things. Not in the study itself.
For this religion is a system of knowledge;
Points may be one by one abandoned, but not the study.
Does he preach passion and non-violence?
Yes, and trees, crops, children honestly taught. He says:
Prepare yourselves for suffering.

Now the rule closes in, the last things are forbidden.
There is no real survival without these.
Now it is time for prison and the unknown.
The old man flowers into spiritual fire.

Streaking of agony across the sky.
Torn black. Red racing on blackness. Dawn.
Rufus looks at him over the rakes of death
Asking, "What is it?
Have you magic powers? Or do you feel no pain?"

*
*

The old man answers, "No. But there is a commandment
      saying
Thou shalt love the Lord thy God with all thy heart,
      with all thy soul and with all thy might.
I knew that I loved him with all my heart and might.
Now I know that I love him with all my life."

The look of delight of the martyr
Among the colors of pain, at last knowing his own response
Total and unified.
To love God with all the heart, all passion,
Every desire called evil, turned toward unity,
All the opposites, all in the dialogue.
All the dark and light of the heart, of life made whole.

Surpassing the known life, days and ideas.
My hope, my life, my burst of consciousness:
To confirm my life in the time of confrontation.

The old man saying Shema.
The death of Akiba.

THE WITNESS

Who is the witness? What voice moves across time,
Speaks for the life and death as witness voice?
Moving tonight on this city, this river, my winter street?

*
*

He saw it, the one witness. Tonight the life as legend
Goes building a meeting for me in the veins of night
Adding its scenes and its songs. Here is the man trans-
    formed,

The tall shepherd, the law, the false messiah, all;
You who come after me far from tonight finding
These lives that ask you always Who is the witness —

Take from us acts of encounter we at night
Wake to attempt, as signs, seeds of beginning,
Given from darkness and remembering darkness,

Take from our light given to you our meetings.
Time tells us men and women, tells us You
The witness, your moment covered with signs, your self.

Tells us this moment, saying You are the meeting.
You are made of signs, your eyes and your song.
Your dance the dance, the walk into the present.

All this we are and accept, being made of signs, speaking
To you, in time not yet born.
                              The witness is myself.
                                            And you,
The signs, the journeys of the night, survive.

KÄTHE KOLLWITZ

I

Held between wars
my lifetime
                among wars, the big hands of the world of death
my lifetime
listens to yours.

The faces of the sufferers
in the street, in dailiness,
their lives showing
through their bodies
a look as of music
the revolutionary look
that says   I am in the world
to change the world
my lifetime
is to love to endure to suffer the music
to set its portrait
up as a sheet of the world
the most moving the most alive
Easter and bone
and Faust walking among the flowers of the world
and the child alive within the living woman, music of man,
and death holding my lifetime between great hands
the hands of enduring life

*
*

that suffers the gifts and madness of full life, on earth, in
        our time,
and through my life, through my eyes, through my arms
        and hands
may give the face of this music in portrait waiting for
the unknown person
held in the two hands, you.

II

Woman as gates, saying :
"The process is after all like music,
like the development of a piece of music.
The fugues come back and

                                again and again
interweave.
A theme may seem to have been put aside,
but it keeps returning —
the same thing modulated,
somewhat changed in form.
Usually richer.
And it is very good that this is so."

A woman pouring her opposites.
"After all there are happy things in life too.
Why do you show only the dark side?"
"I could not answer this. But I know —
in the beginning my impulse to know
the working life

        *
    *

             had little to do with
pity or sympathy.
                 I simply felt
that the life of the workers was beautiful."

She said, "I am groping in the dark."

She said, "When the door opens, of sensuality,
then you will understand it too. The struggle begins.
Never again to be free of it,
often you will feel it to be your enemy.
Sometimes
you will almost suffocate,
such joy it brings."

Saying of her husband : "My wish
is to die after Karl.
I know no person who can love as he can,
with his whole soul.
Often this love has oppressed me;
I wanted to be free.
But often too it has made me
so terribly happy."

She said : "We rowed over to Carrara at dawn,
climbed up to the marble quarries
and rowed back at night. The drops of water
fell like glittering stars
from our oars."

   *
*

She said : "As a matter of fact,
I believe
            that bisexuality
is almost   a necessary factor
in artistic production; at any rate,
the tinge of masculinity within me
helped me
            in my work."

She said : "The only technique I can still manage.
It's hardly a technique at all, lithography.
In it
            only the essentials count."

A tight-lipped man in a restaurant last night
            saying to me :
"Kollwitz?   She's too black-and-white."

III

Held among wars, watching
   all of them
   all these people
   weavers,
   Carmagnole

Looking at
   all of them
   death, the children
   patients in waiting-rooms

*
*

famine
the street
the corpse with the baby
floating, on the dark river

A woman seeing
the violent, inexorable
movement of nakedness
and the confession of No
the confession of great weakness, war,
all streaming to one son killed, Peter;
even the son left living; repeated,
the father, the mother; the grandson
another Peter killed in another war; firestorm;
dark, light, as two hands,
this pole and that pole as the gates.

What would happen if one woman told the truth about
    her life?
The world would split open

IV   SONG : THE CALLING-UP

Rumor, stir of ripeness
rising within this girl
sensual blossoming
of meaning, its light and form.

*
*

The birth-cry summoning
out of the male, the father
from the warm woman
a mother in response.

The word of death
calls up the fight with stone
wrestle with grief with time
from the material make
an art harder than bronze.

V   SELF-PORTRAIT

Mouth looking directly at you
eyes in their inwardness looking
directly at you
half light   half darkness
woman, strong, German, young artist
flows into
wide sensual mouth meditating
looking right at you
eyes shadowed with brave hand
looking deep at you
flows into
wounded brave mouth
grieving and hooded eyes
alive, German, in her first War

*
*

flows into
strength of the worn face
a skein of lines
broods, flows into
mothers among the war graves
bent over death
facing the father
stubborn upon the field
flows into
the marks of her knowing —
Nie Wieder Krieg
repeated in the eyes
flows into
"Seedcorn must not be ground"
and the grooved cheek
lips drawn fine
the down-drawn grief
face of our age
flows into
Pieta, mother and
between her knees
life as her son in death
pouring from the sky of
one more war
flows into
face almost obliterated
hand over the mouth forever
hand over one eye now
the other great eye
closed

*
*

V *THE SPEED OF DARKNESS*

THE SPEED OF DARKNESS

I

Whoever despises the clitoris despises the penis
Whoever despises the penis despises the cunt
Whoever despises the cunt despises the life of the child.

Resurrection music,   silence,   and surf.

II

No longer speaking
Listening with the whole body
And with every drop of blood
Overtaken by silence

But this same silence is become speech
With the speed of darkness.

III

Stillness during war, the lake.
The unmoving spruces.
Glints over the water.
Faces, voices.   You are far away.
A tree that trembles.

I am the tree that trembles and trembles.

IV

After the lifting of the mist
after the lift of the heavy rains
the sky stands clear
and the cries of the city risen in day
I remember the buildings are space
walled, to let space be used for living
I mind this room is space
this drinking glass is space
whose boundary of glass
lets me give you drink and space to drink
your hand, my hand being space
containing skies and constellations
your face
carries the reaches of air
I know I am space
my words are air.

V

Between   between
the man : act   exact
woman : in curve   senses in their maze
frail orbits, green tries,   games of stars
shape of the body speaking its evidence

VI

I look across at the real
vulnerable   involved   naked

*
*

devoted to the present of all I care for
the world of its history leading to this moment.

VII

Life the announcer.
I assure you
there are many ways to have a child.
I bastard mother
promise you
there are many ways to be born.
They all come forth
in their own grace.

VIII

Ends of the earth join tonight
with blazing stars upon their meeting.

These sons,   these sons
fall burning into Asia.

IX

Time comes into it.
Say it.   Say it.

The universe is made of stories,
not of atoms.

X

Lying
blazing beside me

*
*

you rear beautifully and up —
your thinking face —
erotic body reaching
in all its colors and lights —
your erotic face
colored and lit —
not colored body-and-face
but now entire,
colors   lights   the world thinking and reaching.

XI

The river flows past the city.

Water goes down to tomorrow
making its children   I hear their unborn voices
I am working out the vocabulary of my silence.

XII

Big-boned man young and of my dream
Struggles to get the live bird out of his throat.
I am he am I?   Dreaming?
I am the bird am I?   I am the throat?

A bird with a curved beak.
It could slit anything, the throat-bird.

Drawn up slowly.   The curved blades, not large.
Bird emerges   wet   being born
Begins to sing.

*
*

XIII

My night awake
staring at the broad rough jewel
the copper roof across the way
thinking of the poet
yet unborn in this dark
who will be the throat of these hours.
No.   Of those hours.
Who will speak these days,
if not I,
if not you?

*
*

ABOUT THE AUTHOR

MURIEL RUKEYSER has published ten volumes of poetry, three books of prose and a number of children's books. Her work has been translated into ten languages. A member of the National Institute of Arts and Letters, Mrs. Rukeyser's poetry has appeared in such magazines as *The New Yorker, The Nation, The Observer, Poetry* and *Atlantic Monthly.* Muriel Rukeyser lives in New York City.